DISCARD

Lodi Memorial Library
One Memorial Dr.
Lodi, NJ   07644-1692

GAYLORD

A Child's Book of Wildflowers

M. A. KELLY
ILLUSTRATED BY JOYCE POWZYK

FOUR WINDS PRESS New York

MAXWELL MACMILLAN CANADA   Toronto

MAXWELL MACMILLAN INTERNATIONAL   New York   Oxford   Singapore   Sydney

PROPERTY OF
LODI MEMORIAL LIBRARY

In loving memory of Margaret and James Kelly

—M. A. K.

This is for you, Henri

—J. P.

Special thanks to Dr. Donald Stratton, at the Department of
Ecology and Evolutionary Biology, Princeton University,
for checking the facts in this book.

LODI MEMORIAL LIBRARY, NJ

3 9139 05018403 6

Text copyright © 1992 by M. A. Kelly
Illustrations copyright © 1992 by Joyce Powzyk

All rights reserved. No part of this book may be reproduced or
transmitted in any form or by any means, electronic or mechanical,
including photocopying, recording, or by any information storage and
retrieval system, without permission in writing from the Publisher.

Four Winds Press   Maxwell Macmillan Canada, Inc.
Macmillan Publishing Company   1200 Eglinton Avenue East
866 Third Avenue   Suite 200
New York, NY 10022   Don Mills, Ontario M3C 3N1

Macmillan Publishing Company is part of the Maxwell Communication
Group of Companies.

First edition
Printed and bound in the United States of America
10   9   8   7   6   5   4   3   2   1

The text of this book is set in Jamille.
Book design by Christy Hale
Calligraphy by Edward R. Heins

Library of Congress Cataloging-in-Publication Data
Kelly, M. A.   A child's book of wildflowers / M. A. Kelly ;
illustrated by Joyce Powzyk. — 1st American ed.
      p.   cm. Summary: Describes a variety of wildflowers,
discussing their appearance, blooming season, and significance
in history and folklore.
ISBN 0-02-750142-6
1. Wild flowers—North America—Juvenile literature. 2. Wild
flowers— Juvenile literature. 3. Wild flowers—Folklore—Juvenile
literature. [1. Wild flowers.] I. Powzyk, Joyce Ann, ill. II. Title.
QK110.K45 1992
582.13—dc20   91-30368

CONTENTS

A NOTE FROM THE AUTHOR

Wildflower facts and fancies are part of the folklore all Americans share, no matter where we live. Those of us who live in the city have, perhaps, a special appreciation for the dandelion growing in a crack in the sidewalk or the Queen Anne's lace blooming in an empty lot. Those of us who live in the suburbs or in the country might be more familiar with a field of clover or a fragrant meadow full of many different wildflowers.

One of the difficulties in writing about wildflowers is that the same name is often used for different species of the same genus of plants. For example, "violet" is the common name for over seventy plants. More confusion is created when the same plant is known by other names in various parts of the country. Thus a flower is called bouncing Bet in one area and soapwort in another.

In this book the wildflowers are identified first by their most common name and then by their generally accepted Latin name. The first word of the Latin name is the name given to a whole group of related plants, the *genus*. The second word, the *species,* refers to the particular plant within the genus group. Some other common names of flowers are also listed.

A wildflower that grows where you live may have a different name, or it may not look exactly like the one pictured in this book. Wildflowers just don't always lend themselves to strict categories. They are, after all, wild!

A NOTE FROM THE ARTIST

The following wildflower paintings were done during the late summer and early autumn. The palette is comprised of colors quite different from those of a spring rendition, emphasizing shades of burnt sienna, sap green, and ochre. Many of the featured flowers had stems that had turned red from age and leaves that were yellowed and riddled with imperfections. Each painting is done with a mixture of Rowney and Winsor & Newton watercolor paints on Fabriano 100% rag paper.

STEP 1
Graphite pencil sketch of the plant and its flower(s), capturing its overall appearance, leaf shape, how it bends, etc., which serve to identify the species.

STEP 2
A black colored pencil is applied over the graphite to emphasize form and to check whether the design is balanced and pleasing to the viewer.

STEP 3
An undercoat of yellow-green watercolor is applied, followed by darker hues of green. Careful attention is paid to the subtleties of these greens; that is, whether they are bluish, brownish, etc. Dark shadows are also added, while areas of light undercoat are left uncovered to give depth to the subject.

STEP 4
A wash is added behind the studies, especially the black pencil study, which has remained uncolored—a technique used to emphasize the plant's conformation (while the watercolor study emphasizes its color).

TOUCH-ME-NOT
Impatiens capensis
Jewelweed, Snapweed

Blooms: Summer to fall
Size: 2 to 5 feet tall;
flower: about 1 inch long
Color: Yellow or orange, with small
dark spots

Touch-me-not is indigenous, or native, to eastern North America. It has spread to the South and the West, growing near ponds and on shady riverbanks.

The touch-me-not flower is shaped like an elf's cap. The long spur in the back is filled with nectar. Bees and hummingbirds flock to touch-me-nots in search of this nectar. The plant is called touch-me-not because its ripe seed pods explode at the slightest touch and shoot their seeds out three or four feet.

Native Americans used the touch-me-not plant to soothe the rash of poison ivy.

To do: For generations children have loved pinching ripe touch-me-not seed pods. Even though you are expecting it, you will be startled when the seeds pop out at you.

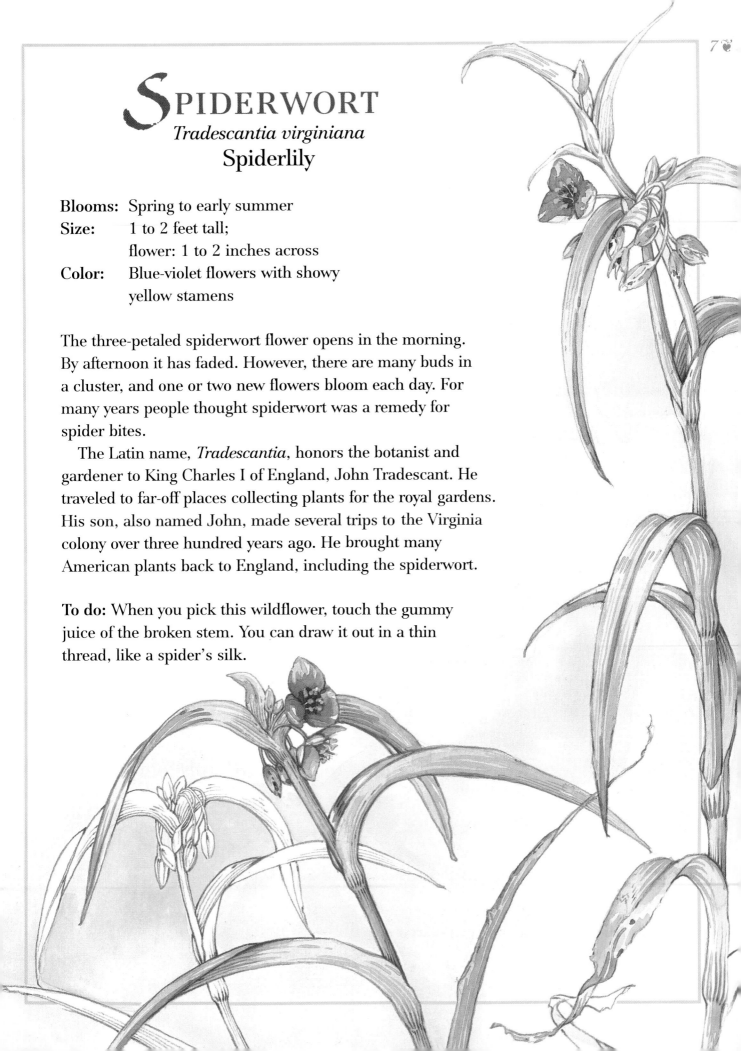

SPIDERWORT
Tradescantia virginiana
Spiderlily

Blooms: Spring to early summer
Size: 1 to 2 feet tall;
 flower: 1 to 2 inches across
Color: Blue-violet flowers with showy
 yellow stamens

The three-petaled spiderwort flower opens in the morning.
By afternoon it has faded. However, there are many buds in
a cluster, and one or two new flowers bloom each day. For
many years people thought spiderwort was a remedy for
spider bites.

 The Latin name, *Tradescantia*, honors the botanist and
gardener to King Charles I of England, John Tradescant. He
traveled to far-off places collecting plants for the royal gardens.
His son, also named John, made several trips to the Virginia
colony over three hundred years ago. He brought many
American plants back to England, including the spiderwort.

To do: When you pick this wildflower, touch the gummy
juice of the broken stem. You can draw it out in a thin
thread, like a spider's silk.

MULLEIN

Verbascum thapsus

Velvet Plant, Flannel Leaf, High Taper

Blooms: Early summer to early fall
Size: 2 to 6 or more feet tall; flower: about 1 inch across
Color: Yellow flowers; gray-green leaves and stem

Early settlers brought mullein with them from Europe for use as a medicinal herb. Now it is found all over North America.

The plant lives just two years. The first year, there is a large rosette of furry leaves. Some leaves may be over a foot long. The second year, the plant sends up a thick leafy stem topped with a spike of yellow flowers. The flowers bloom a few at a time. Tiny hairs cover the entire plant, giving it a velvety look and feel.

Mullein is a plant of many uses. Ancient Romans dipped dried mullein stalks in melted fat and burned them as torches. Native Americans and early settlers lined their moccasins and shoes with mullein leaves to keep their feet warm. Some Native American mothers used mullein leaves to diaper their babies.

To do: The first year's growth of mullein stays green right through the winter. Try wrapping big leaves around your ankles and under your socks on a cold day the way Native Americans and colonists did.

Sunflower
Helianthus annuus

Blooms: Summer and fall
Size: 2 to 10 feet tall;
flower head: 4 to 6 inches across
Color: Yellow ''petals''; dark orange to
red centers

When the sun rises in the east, the faces of the sunflowers are still turned to the west, where the sun had set. Within half an hour after sunrise, the flowers again have turned their faces toward the sun. They follow it through the day from east to west.

Sunflowers are indigenous to the Western Hemisphere. Since remote times, Native Americans have cultivated sunflowers, eaten the seeds, and boiled them to extract oil. The Incas of Peru revered this flower as sacred to their sun god.

The citizens of Kansas love the sunflower so much, they have made it their state flower.

To do: Plant some sunflower seeds. Long before the flower heads develop, you will be able to observe the fast-growing seedlings leaning toward the sun.

YARROW
Achillea lanulosa and
Achillea millefolium
Milfoil, Thousand Leaf,
Soldier's Woundwort

Blooms: Summer to fall
Size: 1 to 2 feet tall;
           flowers: tiny in a flat-topped
           cluster 2 to 3 inches across
Color: White or white tinged with pink

Yarrow is found all over the world. The indigenous American yarrow (*A. lanulosa*) and the European import (*A. millefolium*) are so alike that only a botanist using a microscope can distinguish one from the other.

The Latin name honors Achilles, an ancient Greek hero. Achilles used the plant to heal the wounds of his soldiers during the Trojan War. Doctors were still using yarrow to heal wounds during the American Civil War. Yarrow does, in fact, contain a substance that helps stop bleeding.

The word *millefolium* is Latin for "a thousand leaves." It refers to the plant's lacy foliage, which is made up of countless tiny leaflets.

To do: Like many plants with a long history, yarrow was used in charms. The belief was that if you put some yarrow under your pillow before you went to bed, you would see your future husband or wife in a dream.

ST. JOHNSWORT
Hypericum perforatum

Blooms: Summer to early fall
Size: 2 feet or more;
        flower: 1 inch or less across
Color: Golden yellow

There are more than two dozen species of St. Johnswort native to America, but this one, brought here from Europe, is the most common. Along the edges of its petals are tiny black dots—these are resin-containing glands. The leaves are dotted with oil glands. From ancient times until the twentieth century, both oil and resin from this herb were used in medicine, especially for soothing and healing wounds.

For centuries country folk all over Europe gathered St. Johnswort on June 23, the eve of the feast of St. John the Baptist, from whom this plant gets its name. This is also the eve of Midsummer Day. Long ago people believed that Midsummer Eve was a time of magic when fairies and spirits roamed. St. Johnswort, with its healing properties, was considered a good luck charm and a protection against evil spirits.

To do: Hold a St. Johnswort leaf in front of a light. You will see the light shining through the tiny translucent oil glands. The glands look like perforations or holes, giving the species its name, *perforatum.*

DANDELION
Taraxacum officinale

Blooms: Early spring until frost
Size: 3 to 14 inches tall;
flower head: about 1½ inches across
Color: Bright yellow

Early settlers from Europe, who valued the dandelion for food and medicine, brought it to America and cultivated it in their gardens. Today most people consider the dandelion just a lawn pest.

The dandelion gets its name from the French *dent de lion*, or "lion's tooth." The jagged edges of the leaves have been compared with the teeth of a lion.

Dandelions are very sensitive to sunlight. They open early on sunny days and close at sunset. They even close on overcast days when rain threatens.

To do: People in Ireland use the milky juice of the dandelion stem to remove warts. If you have a wart, you might try this cure to see if it works.

Dandelion Seed Head
Puffball, Blowball, Clockflower, Fairy Clock

Dandelion plants may have seed heads, flowers, and buds all at the same time. Each of the two hundred or more florets of a flower head produces a seed, which is attached to silky fibers. A puff of wind can send these many seeds flying—perhaps to land, take root, and produce more dandelions.

To do: Here are three traditions connected with dandelion puffballs.

Blow all the seeds away. The number of puffs it takes to send them all flying is the hour of the day—at least in fairyland.

Blow on the puffball as hard as you can. The number of seeds left is the number of children you will have.

Make a wish. Blow on the seed head as hard as you can. If all the seeds fly off, your wish will come true.

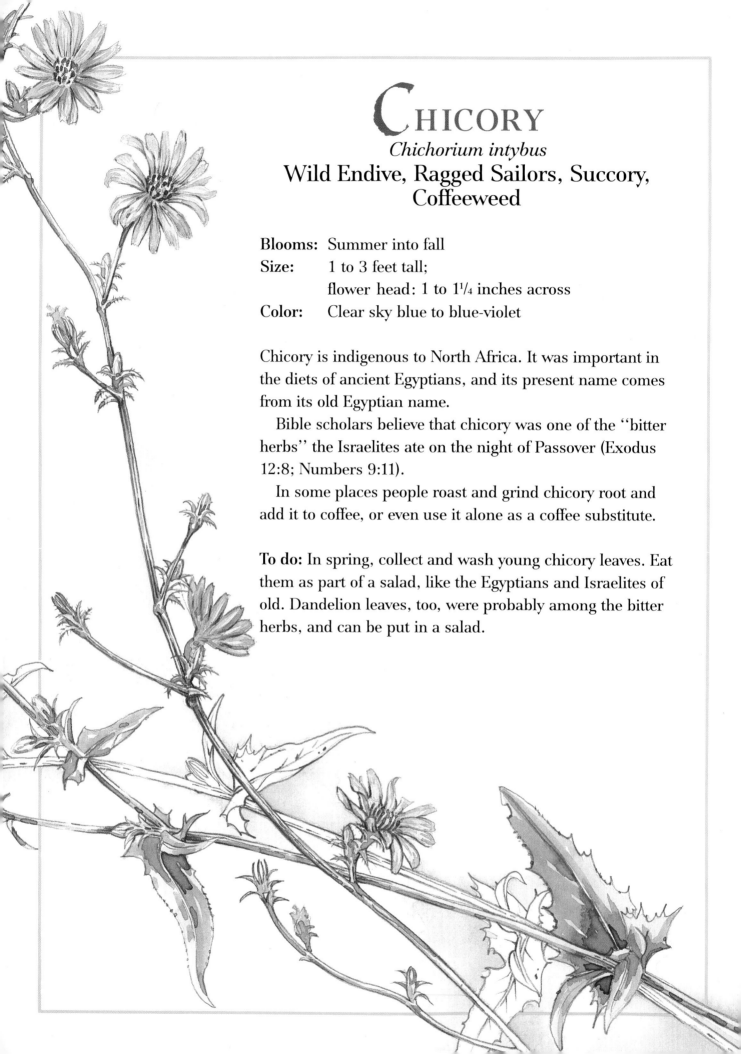

CHICORY

Chichorium intybus

Wild Endive, Ragged Sailors, Succory, Coffeeweed

Blooms: Summer into fall
Size: 1 to 3 feet tall;
flower head: 1 to 1¼ inches across
Color: Clear sky blue to blue-violet

Chicory is indigenous to North Africa. It was important in the diets of ancient Egyptians, and its present name comes from its old Egyptian name.

Bible scholars believe that chicory was one of the "bitter herbs" the Israelites ate on the night of Passover (Exodus 12:8; Numbers 9:11).

In some places people roast and grind chicory root and add it to coffee, or even use it alone as a coffee substitute.

To do: In spring, collect and wash young chicory leaves. Eat them as part of a salad, like the Egyptians and Israelites of old. Dandelion leaves, too, were probably among the bitter herbs, and can be put in a salad.

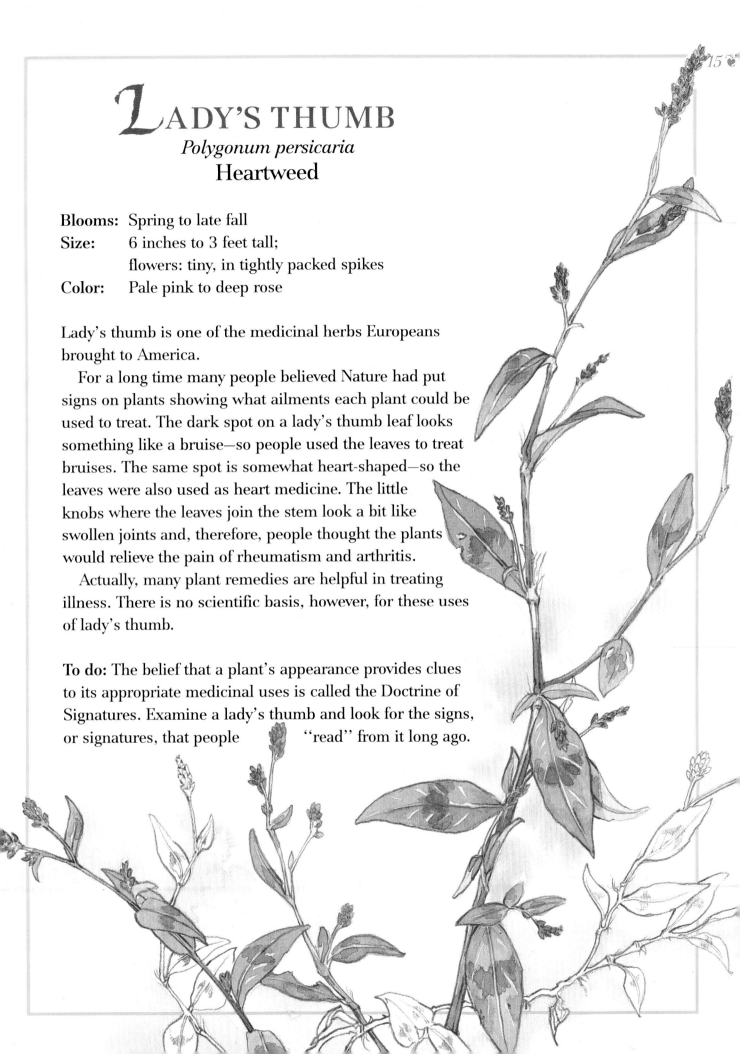

LADY'S THUMB
Polygonum persicaria
Heartweed

Blooms: Spring to late fall
Size: 6 inches to 3 feet tall;
flowers: tiny, in tightly packed spikes
Color: Pale pink to deep rose

Lady's thumb is one of the medicinal herbs Europeans brought to America.

For a long time many people believed Nature had put signs on plants showing what ailments each plant could be used to treat. The dark spot on a lady's thumb leaf looks something like a bruise—so people used the leaves to treat bruises. The same spot is somewhat heart-shaped—so the leaves were also used as heart medicine. The little knobs where the leaves join the stem look a bit like swollen joints and, therefore, people thought the plants would relieve the pain of rheumatism and arthritis.

Actually, many plant remedies are helpful in treating illness. There is no scientific basis, however, for these uses of lady's thumb.

To do: The belief that a plant's appearance provides clues to its appropriate medicinal uses is called the Doctrine of Signatures. Examine a lady's thumb and look for the signs, or signatures, that people "read" from it long ago.

QUEEN ANNE'S LACE
Daucus carota
Wild Carrot, Laceflower

Blooms: Spring through summer
Size: 1 to 4 feet tall;
flower umbel: $2^1/_2$ to
6 inches across
Color: White, often with a purple
floweret in center

Queen Anne's lace is the wild ancestor of the carrot. In ancient times, by selection and cultivation, farmers developed the sweet orange carrot from the stringy white root of this plant.

According to legend, Queen Anne of England and the ladies of her court decorated their hair and clothes with these flowers.

Colonists brought Queen Anne's lace to America as both a garden flower and a medicinal herb.

To do: You can tint Queen Anne's lace (or other white flowers). Mix food coloring in a small amount of warm water, just enough to cover an inch or so of the stems. Twenty-four hours later, when the plants have absorbed the colored water, the flowers should be nicely tinted. Discard the dye and put your flowers in a vase with clear water.

MILKWEED
Asclepias syriaca
Silkweed, Wild Cotton

Blooms: Summer
Size: 3 to 6 feet tall;
            flowers: ½ inch across,
            in clusters 2 inches wide
Color: Dull lavender, purplish pink

In the fall, milkweed forms large pods packed with seeds. Each seed is attached to silky fibers. With these "parachutes," milkweed seeds float off on the wind.

People have used milkweed "silk" to make paper, felt, and cloth. Early settlers stuffed quilts, pillows, and mattresses with it. During World War I, children were paid a penny a pod to collect milkweed silk for use as filling for life jackets.

The monarch butterfly belongs to a family called "milkweed butterflies" because of their dependence on the milkweed plant. The butterflies feed on milkweed nectar. They lay their eggs on the plants, and monarch caterpillars grow and feed on the milkweed leaves.

To do: Early settlers used the sticky white milkweed juice as glue. You can use it to glue pressed flowers to notepaper. (See *Violet* for pressing instructions.) Select a milkweed plant with lots of leaves. Cut or pull off the leaves as you need them. Use the stem of the leaf to dab drops of juice on the paper. Arrange pressed flowers on the glue.

GOLDENROD
Solidago canadensis

Blooms: Late summer through fall
Size: 1 to 4 feet tall;
flower cluster: 2 to 15 inches long
Color: Golden yellow

Goldenrods belong to the genus *Solidago.* *Solidago* is from the Latin *solido,* meaning "to make whole," in the sense of "to make whole or well." For centuries, herbalists throughout the world treated a variety of ailments with medicine made from goldenrod.

There are more than sixty species of goldenrod growing throughout the United States. Some of them are native, and some were brought over from Europe. Almost all varieties have tiny golden flowers growing in large showy clusters.

At one time many people believed that the pollen from goldenrod caused hay fever. Now we know that the real culprit is ragweed, which comes into bloom at the same time.

To do: Goldenrod is one of the best wild-flowers for air-drying. Pick a large bunch, tie the stems together with a rubber band, and hang them in a cool, airy place. They should be dry in about two weeks and ready to display all winter.

BUTTERCUP
Ranunculus acris

Blooms: Spring through summer
Size: 1 to 3 feet tall;
flower: almost 1 inch across
Color: Shiny yellow

Farmers regard buttercups as pests, because they contain an acrid juice that can sicken cattle.

European settlers chose to bring many seeds to America in order to grow plants for food, for medicine, or just for beauty. They did *not* want to bring buttercup seeds. But the unwanted buttercup seeds came anyway. They may have been mixed in with grass or other crop seeds. Perhaps some came in packing material or on the hooves of animals or stuck to clothes and luggage. The seeds took root in American soil, and buttercups spread all over the land.

To do: Find out whether your friends like butter. Hold a buttercup under a friend's chin. If you can detect a yellow glow, your friend likes butter. Perhaps your parents and grandparents have played this game, too.

Be careful not to crush the flowers, stems, or leaves. The entire plant contains an acrid juice that can irritate and even blister your skin.

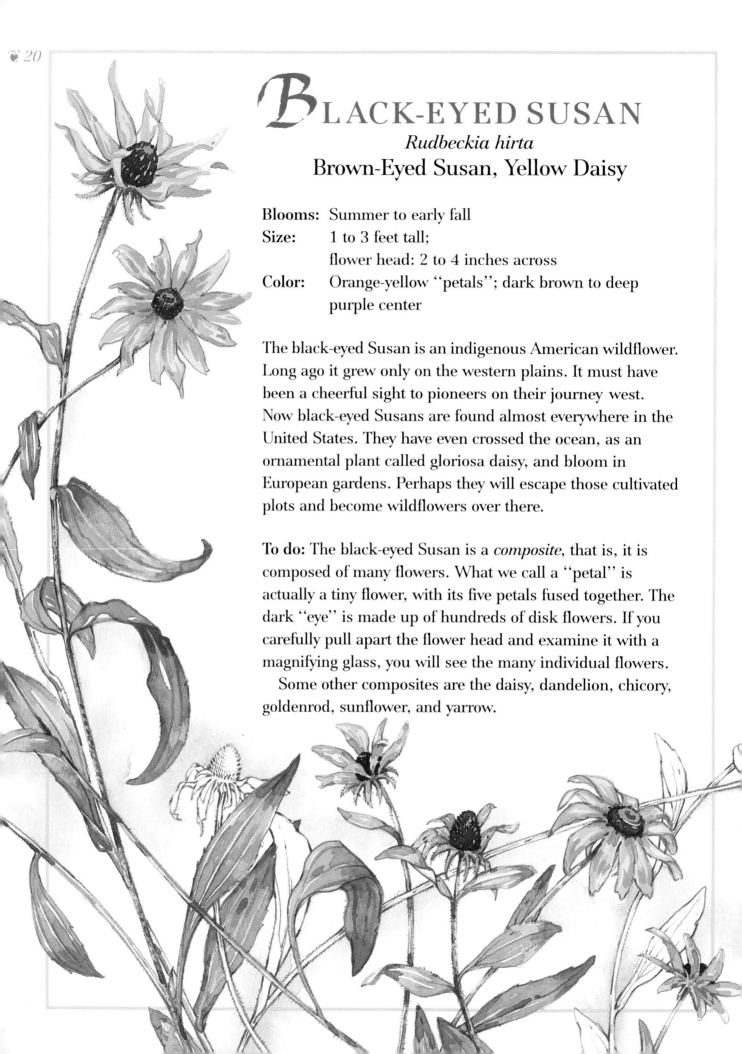

BLACK-EYED SUSAN
Rudbeckia hirta
Brown-Eyed Susan, Yellow Daisy

Blooms: Summer to early fall
Size: 1 to 3 feet tall;
            flower head: 2 to 4 inches across
Color: Orange-yellow ''petals''; dark brown to deep
            purple center

The black-eyed Susan is an indigenous American wildflower. Long ago it grew only on the western plains. It must have been a cheerful sight to pioneers on their journey west. Now black-eyed Susans are found almost everywhere in the United States. They have even crossed the ocean, as an ornamental plant called gloriosa daisy, and bloom in European gardens. Perhaps they will escape those cultivated plots and become wildflowers over there.

To do: The black-eyed Susan is a *composite*, that is, it is composed of many flowers. What we call a ''petal'' is actually a tiny flower, with its five petals fused together. The dark ''eye'' is made up of hundreds of disk flowers. If you carefully pull apart the flower head and examine it with a magnifying glass, you will see the many individual flowers.

Some other composites are the daisy, dandelion, chicory, goldenrod, sunflower, and yarrow.

DAISY

Chrysanthemum leucanthemum

Ox-Eye Daisy, Field Daisy, Marguerite

Blooms: Summer

Size: 1 to 3 feet tall;
flower head: 1 to 2 inches across

Color: Snow-white "petals"; golden center

Daisies grow all over North America, but they are not native wildflowers. European settlers carried daisy seeds to America. Some seeds were brought intentionally, for growing garden flowers, but most daisy seeds came here by accident, mixed in with grass and other crop seeds.

The name *daisy* comes from an old form of the words "day's eye."

Daisies do not wilt quickly after they are picked. Perhaps that's what led to the expression "fresh as a daisy." A bouquet of daisies will stay fresh in water for almost two weeks. Children often make slits in the stems and link the flowers together to form daisy chains, necklaces, and crowns that stay perky without water for several hours.

To do: As children have been doing for centuries, you, too, can pluck the "petals" and ask the daisy if a certain someone loves you or not. The last "petal" gives the answer.

POKEWEED
Phytolacca americana
Inkberry, Pokeberry, Pigeonberry

Blooms: Late summer to fall

Size: 4 to 10 feet tall;
small flowers on droopy spikes 4 to 6 inches long

Color: White flowers; red or purple stem; dark purple berries

As the botanical name (*Phytolacca americana*) indicates, pokeweed is an indigenous American plant. Its common name is also of native origin. ''Poke'' comes from the Virginia Algonquian word for blood and refers to the red color of the stem, branches, and berry juice. Native Americans made a red dye from the berries. Colonists used them to make ink, which accounts for one of the plant's other names, inkberry. Some birds eat the berries, and hence, yet another name—pigeonberry. However, the whole plant, including the berries, is poisonous to people.

To do: The celebrated American artist George Caleb Bingham (1811–1879) made a beautiful, deep pink pigment from pokeweed berries to use in some of his work. You, too, can paint with pokeweed berry juice. Strip the berries into a small bowl or cup. Crush them with the back of a spoon. Dip your paintbrush into the juice and paint.

MINT

Mentha arvensis	*Mentha spicata*	*Mentha piperita*
Field Mint	**Spearmint**	**Peppermint**

Blooms: Summer to early fall
Size: 1 to 2 feet tall;
flower: very small
Color: Pale lilac or white

Mint grows all over the world. From earliest times people have used mint in preparing medicines and flavoring foods. Ancient Greeks liked to scent their bathwater with mint.

Field mint is the only indigenous American mint. Spearmint and peppermint are immigrants from Europe. Now they grow wild throughout the country. You can recognize mint by its clusters of tiny flowers, square stems, and fragrant odor. Small glands containing strongly scented oil cover the leaves. Pinching or crushing the leaves releases a delightful fragrance. It may remind you of toothpaste, chewing gum, or candy canes. That's because mint oil is used in preparing them.

To do: For a refreshing summer bath, add mint to the water. Put a bunch of fresh mint into a sock and seal it with a rubber band. Twist and roll the sock to crush the leaves. Toss it into the tub and run the water.

VIOLET
Viola papilionacea
Common Blue Violet

Blooms: Spring through early summer
Size: 3 to 8 inches tall;
flower: $^3/_4$ inch across
Color: Deep purple with a white throat

There are hundreds of species of violet all over the world, including seventy-seven different ones in North America. Some violets are white or yellow, but most are shades of violet. The common blue violet isn't blue at all. It is a deep, rich purple.
　In the language of flowers, the violet is the symbol of modesty and shyness.

To do: For centuries botanists have preserved flowers by pressing. Press the flowers as soon as possible after picking. Place a piece of absorbent paper on a flat surface and arrange the flowers and leaves on it. Cover them with another piece of absorbent paper and weigh them down with books or the like. Do not disturb for at least a week. Dried flowers keep indefinitely.

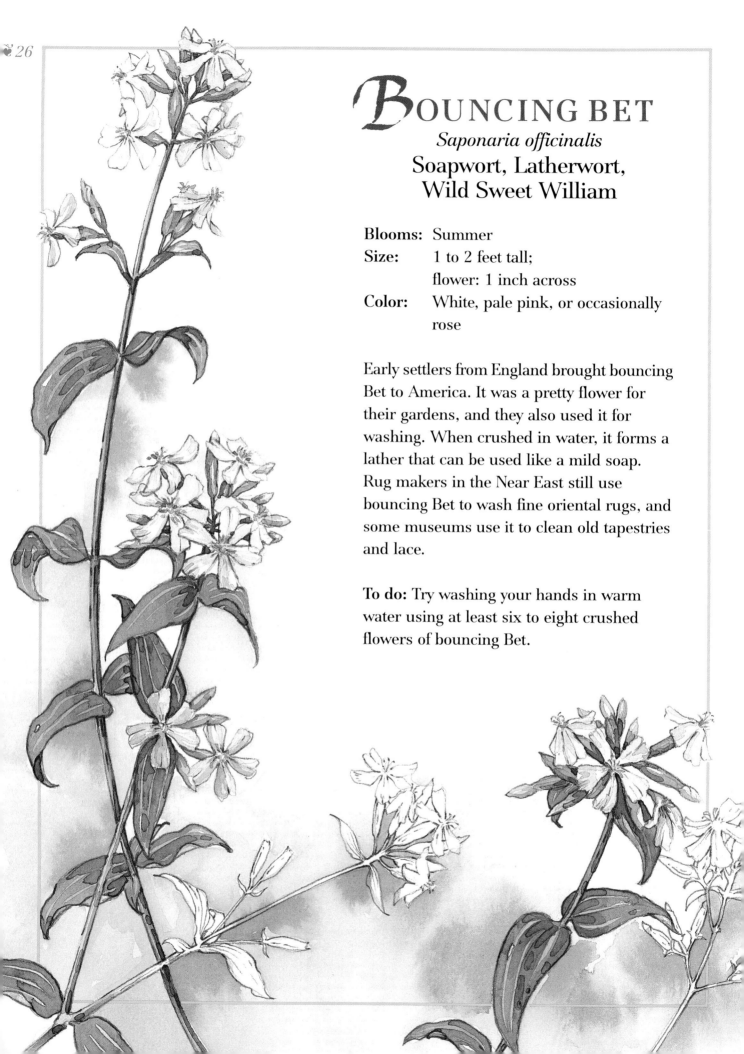

BOUNCING BET
Saponaria officinalis
Soapwort, Latherwort, Wild Sweet William

Blooms: Summer
Size: 1 to 2 feet tall;
flower: 1 inch across
Color: White, pale pink, or occasionally rose

Early settlers from England brought bouncing Bet to America. It was a pretty flower for their gardens, and they also used it for washing. When crushed in water, it forms a lather that can be used like a mild soap. Rug makers in the Near East still use bouncing Bet to wash fine oriental rugs, and some museums use it to clean old tapestries and lace.

To do: Try washing your hands in warm water using at least six to eight crushed flowers of bouncing Bet.

CLOVER

Trifolium repens
White Clover

Trifolium pratense
Red Clover

Blooms: Late spring to early fall

Size: *White:* 3 to 6 inches tall;
                flower head: ¾ inch across
      Red: 4 to 12 inches tall;
                flower head: up to an inch across

Color: *White:* Creamy white with occasional hint of pink
      Red: From delicate, pale pink to deep
              magenta purple

Settlers from Europe brought seeds of both red and white clovers to America. Now these clovers grow all across the country. Farmers value clover because it enriches the soil. Honeybees seem to work white clover longer than any other flower and they produce excellent honey from its nectar. Bumblebees prefer red clover.

Long ago, clover was used in medicines to treat a number of different ailments. Many thought the plant had magical powers. Even today there are people who think that finding a four-leaf clover means that they will have good luck.

To do: Clover leaves are divided into three leaflets. Four-leaf clovers are rare, but they can be found if you look hard enough. Good luck!

BLACKBERRY

Rubus species
Bramble

Blooms: Late spring to early summer; fruit ripens late summer
Size: Canes up to 6 feet long;
flower: about 1 inch across
Color: White or pale pink

There are over two hundred different species of blackberry growing all over North America. The stems are called canes. Some are low and trailing, while others are tall and stiff. Almost all of them have thorns or prickles.

Rabbits, mice, and birds often make their nests under or in blackberry bushes, protected from their enemies by the tangle of thorny canes.

When Sleeping Beauty fell asleep for one hundred years in fulfillment of the evil witch's curse, a wall of bramble (that is, blackberry) sprang up around the castle. The thorny hedge kept out all who tried to enter, until the prince came. Then the brambles opened before him. He found Sleeping Beauty and awakened her with a kiss.

To do: Pick and eat blackberries. They are delicious plain or with cream and sugar.

PROPERTY OF
LODI MEMORIAL LIBRARY

BUTTER-AND-EGGS

Linaria vulgaris

Wild Snapdragon, Yellow Toadflax

Blooms: Summer to fall
Size: About 1 foot tall;
flower: 1 to 1½ inches long
Color: Two-toned pale yellow and orange

Butter-and-eggs is one of those special plants that can be pollinated only by a particular insect. For butter-and-eggs, it is the bee. No butterfly or tiny insect can sip the nectar of butter-and-eggs. The flower remains tightly closed until a honeybee or bumblebee lands on the orange spot of the flower's lower lip. The weight of the bee opens the flower, and the bee enters it to get nectar. When the bee comes out, its back is covered with pollen, and it flies on from flower to flower, each time cross-pollinating the flowers.

Colonists brought butter-and-eggs from Europe for use as a garden flower and medicinal herb. The yellow and orange of the flowers account for the plant's name.

To do: Pinch the "jaws" of a butter-and-eggs flower and its mouth will open and close like a dragon's.

EVENING PRIMROSE

Oenothera biennis
Field Primrose

Blooms: Summer to fall
Size: 1 to 6 feet tall;
           flower: 1 to 2 inches across
Color: Bright yellow

The evening primrose, an indigenous American plant, is not very pretty during the day. Wilted flowers and many tightly closed buds top a tall, rough-leaved stem. But as the day fades, the evening primrose blooms. Just before the sun goes down, several clear yellow buds open and their lemon scent perfumes the air. Each beautiful flower lives for just one night.

Late in the season, after the plant has set enough seed, the evening primrose may reverse this pattern. Then the flowers may bloom in the daytime and wilt at night.

To do: Locate an evening primrose during the day so you can find it in the early evening. If you watch carefully, you may catch the flowers opening. The buds unfold quickly, so quickly some people claim you can actually hear the petals spring open. You might also see one of the night-flying moths that pollinate the plant.

WILD ROSE
Rosa species
Pasture Rose, Cherokee Rose, Beach Rose, Swamp Rose, Carolina Rose, Prairie Rose, Virginia Rose

Blooms: Spring and early summer
Size: 2 to 7 feet tall;
flower: 1¼ to 3 inches across
Color: Red, white, or pink

Fossil remains show that wild roses bloomed in the American West over 32 million years ago. More than one hundred species of native wild roses greeted the first immigrants to North America. Colonists used wild rose petals in traditional recipes for medicines and cosmetics. And they ate the vitamin-rich rose hips.

Unlike garden roses, with their many layers of petals, most wild roses have only five petals. Almost all wild roses are very fragrant.

The wild rose is the state flower of Georgia, Iowa, New York, and North Dakota, as well as of the Canadian province of Alberta.

To do: Roses are one of the few flowers that keep their scent after drying. To make a fragrant sachet, pick roses early in the day. Spread the petals in a single layer to dry. Gather the dried petals into a lightweight piece of cloth and tie with a ribbon.